There's a Scar On My Brain

There's a Scar On My Brain

THERESA LILLY

ASA PUBLISHING CORPORATION
AN INNOVATIVE OUTSOURCE BOOK PUBLISHING HYBRID

BBB
100 YEARS
Advancing Trust Together₁ₘ

ASA Publishing Corporation
An Accredited Hybrid Publishing House with the BBB
www.asapublishingcorporation.com

1285 N. Telegraph Rd., PMB 351, Monroe, Michigan 48162

Prelude

Set against the backdrop of Detroit in the 1960s and 70s, the narrative unfolds with vivid descriptions of the city's changing landscape and the challenges faced by the Lilly family.

Theresa's early years are marked by the struggle to find stability in a new home on Detroit's Westside, where her family faces the harsh realities of poverty and domestic violence. Her father's anger and abusive behavior cast a shadow over her childhood, leaving her and her brother Meekie to endure cold nights and frequent illnesses. Despite these hardships, moments of tenderness from her father provide fleeting glimpses of hope.

As Theresa grows older, she navigates the complexities of adolescence, including a youth pregnancy that leads to a harrowing confrontation with her father. The memoir delves into her experiences with relationships, including the abusive dynamics with Justus, a man she meets in her teenage years. Theresa's journey takes her from Detroit to New York City, where she seeks refuge with her brother and begins to rebuild her life.

The narrative is filled with raw and emotional moments, from the beatings and betrayals to the fleeting moments of joy and friendship. Theresa's resilience shines through as she faces the challenges of adulthood, including encounters with the FBI and the relentless pursuit of justice. Her story is a testament to the strength of the human spirit and the power of hope in the face of adversity.

This is her story . . .

Table of Contents

Prelude .... (a)

My Childhood On West Grand Avenue 1

A Youth Pregnancy.. 8

Moving and Meeting... 13

Deeper into the Streets 25

Leaving the State 28

Crossing the Street in New York Can Bring Trouble ... 36

A Minute of Romance... 42

I'm Not the Enemy 50

I Know Things Will Get Better................................... 59

There's a Scar On My Brain

THERESA LILLY

My Childhood

On West Grand Avenue

In 1960, the City of Detroit was undergoing major development. On the Eastside, near Townsend and Charlevoix, the city acquired a two-block radius of homes, intending to build an elementary school. This initiative gave my parents a chance to move beyond the predominantly Black neighborhoods we had lived in.

While searching for a new home, my father discovered a charming three-family flat on Detroit's Westside. The neighborhood was picturesque, with tall trees swaying gracefully in the breeze. My dad secured the house, renting out the two upstairs apartments while our family occupied the spacious downstairs unit. It was a smart move. The city compensated us for relocating, and the rental income from the upstairs tenants not only covered the mortgage but left us with some extra cash each month.

Once I started school, my mom took on a job to help our family thrive. Life seemed to be improving, but our house came with its challenges. We relied on a coal furnace to heat the home, which meant warming two floors. To save costs, Dad turned off the bedroom radiators downstairs, hoping the heat from the rest of the house would rise. Unfortunately, this left my brother Meekie and me enduring cold nights. Despite bundling up in thick pajamas, drafts crept in through poorly sealed windows. It didn't help that the coal furnace aggravated my mom's asthma. As a result, I often fell ill, battling colds three or four times a year.

When things finally felt settled, my parents began leaving me home from school some days. Their instructions were clear: "Stay in bed, and don't open the door for anyone—even if you know them."

When I was five, I caught my first glimpse of the harsh reality that would shape my childhood. Dad would come home from work, his anger palpable. "Meekie and Theresa, go to your rooms and stay there," he'd command. Fear gripped us as we listened to the heavy slaps and the sickening sound of flesh meeting flesh, followed by my mom's cries and desperate yells. I was terrified, angry, and confused. But curiosity got the better of me.

One evening, I grabbed my fishbowl from my dresser and cracked open my bedroom door, pretending to head to the bathroom across the hall. I stood halfway in the hallway, straining to see what was happening to my mom. That's when I heard my dad's voice, sharp and menacing: "Who's out of their bedroom?"

"It's me, Daddy," I replied, my voice trembling.

In an instant, he stormed over, dragging me back into my room. He flung me onto my bed like a ragdoll, yelling and screaming that I should never disobey him again. Across the hall, my brother Meekie stayed silent, too scared to make a sound, knowing he could be next. After what felt like an eternity, Dad shrugged off his rage, grabbed his keys, and stormed out of the house.

"All right, you can come out now," Mom said, her voice shaky but composed.

Meekie and I emerged from our rooms, only to be met with a devastating sight—Mom's eye swollen and bruised. We cried together, overwhelmed by the pain and helplessness. This became a grim routine. Mom often wore dark green cat-eye sunglasses to work, hiding the evidence of Dad's fury. She worked until 4:00 PM every day, while Dad's shift ended at 2:30.

Despite his anger, there were moments when Dad showed a softer side. Whenever I had a cold, he'd rush home to care for me before Mom returned. He'd toast buttered white bread in a frying pan, open a can of tomato soup, and bring it to my room. The soup, with its strange gray and cream-colored bubbles, wasn't exactly appetizing, but I learned to eat it. He'd pull up a chair and spoon-feed me, a fleeting gesture of tenderness in an otherwise turbulent world.

"What are these big white bubbles floating in the soup?" I asked Dad.

"They are oysters," Dad replied.

"Oysters, what are they?"

"They will give you gism."

"What is gism?" I asked.

"You will know when you get older," he

told me.

The oysters didn't wait until I got older, it seemed like they became active in my system right then. Dad would feed me oysters four or five times per year. People say that children can't feel or judge anything until adolescence, but this is not true. I started acting out even in kindergarten.

School was rough, and I had these feelings tingling in certain places I couldn't explain since I didn't know the difference between boys and girls. I only knew we were different because I had a brother, and other people had sisters. I couldn't explain why I wanted to look underneath the bathroom stall at another girl in kindergarten, especially this particular one named Rhonda Gail.

The teacher would call a bathroom break when the bell rang, and I would follow Rhonda into the bathroom. I would go into the stall next to hers and wait for her panties to drop down to her ankles with the inside tags touching the cold floor. Then, I would peep my head under the divider wall. One time, Rhonda caught me peeping at her and told me to stop, but I couldn't. She probably told her mom, because one day she said to me, "If you do that one more time, I am going to also tell the teacher on you." I hated to stop this, but I did.

To this day, I owe Rhonda Gail an apology. My behavior was inexcusable. You should not have to run home from school being chased by another girl, especially in kindergarten.

A Youth Pregnancy

In 1971, on my way to the store, I crossed paths with an older man, likely in his 30s or 40s, driving a sleek Lincoln Continental Mark III. I told him I was 18, and soon we began exchanging numbers and meeting up regularly. Before long, I found myself pregnant. Breaking the news to my parents unleashed chaos—my mom bore the brunt of my father's fury.

As my dad unleashed a relentless beating on her, I couldn't stand by any longer. I grabbed him by the collar and yanked him off her. She was left with a deep cut on her shoulder from the box-spring mattress, along with other bruises and scratches. Later in life, she would tell me that God allowed the pregnancy to happen so she could finally take action to protect her family.

At the time, Roe v. Wade hadn't yet become law. My father found a doctor willing to perform a D&C to terminate the pregnancy. While I was in the hospital, my mom stopped by after work, visibly terrified. She knew going home meant facing another beating. I begged her, "Don't go home. Go to a relative's house." But she shook her head. "No, I've got to go home," she said.

That evening, she made a decision to fight back. Before my dad returned, she emptied a small box of Tide detergent and packed it with her car keys, bank book, wallet, and a gun. She slid the box behind the sofa, ready for what might come. When Dad arrived, he knocked her to the floor and began beating her with his fists. But this time, she was prepared. Reaching into her bra, she pulled out a large ice pick. Startled, he ran to the bedroom to grab his gun. Seizing the moment, she grabbed the Tide box and fled out the front door, driving to a cousin's house with nothing but the clothes on her back.

I had only the clothes I wore to the hospital. My brother Meekie, who had been living with our aunt in Syracuse, New York, came home to join us. For about a month, the three of us stayed with a cousin, though it was cramped with her own family there. Eventually, we moved into her brother's attic—a small space in a one-bedroom house with a half bath upstairs.

One night, around 2:00 AM, we were jolted awake by the sound of fire trucks. Outside, flames engulfed a boarded-up house across the street, sending thick, acrid smoke into the air. The neighborhood was abuzz, with people gathering and news crews from Channels 2, 4, and 7 reporting on the scene. The word "arson" was whispered among the crowd—it was clear the fire had been deliberately set. Shaken, we eventually returned to bed, though the unease lingered.

About a month later, I went to see my dad. While visiting him, I asked, "Did you see the fire on the news?" He said, "No, what fire?"

"The one on Keating Street," I told him. "It was on TV."

"No," he said.

"It was the house across the street where we live." I told him they had pulled the body of a 16-year-old girl from the rubble a couple days ago.

"What? That was a threat to our family." He must have said this because I was 15 at the time. "Wait right here," he told me. He came back from his bedroom and handed me an ice pick. "Do you walk to the bus stop in the dark?"

"Yes," I said.

"If someone is coming toward you, go

across the street. Make sure you look behind you. If that person crosses the street, run up to someone's porch screaming. If they follow you on the porch, knock hard or tear the door down. Take the ice pick and if you must, stab them and keep stabbing them until no life is left. Do you understand me?" He spoke. "I don't care if they are black or white, you keep stabbing them. I will come and pick you up from the police station. Now go home and take care of your mother and brother."

"Yes, Daddy, I understand," I told him.

Moving and Meeting

Not long after leaving Keating, we moved to Fullerton Street on Detroit's Westside, where we stayed for about a year. While living there, I met LaToya Williams, a young woman a couple of years older than me who lived in Highland Park. She introduced me to her friends, Sheila and Cynthia, who also lived in Highland Park. The four of us became fast friends. They quickly learned I was a budding seamstress, crafting almost everything I wore—a necessity since we relied on weekly child support payments and Mom's low-paying job.

One day, when I was 15, my girlfriends and I were driving down Wyoming Street. We passed by a club called The Casino Royal and noticed a sleek white Rolls-Royce parked out front. A Black man stepped out of the car, and I couldn't resist getting out to introduce myself.

"Could I take a picture with your car?" I asked. I told him I was a seamstress and had made the outfit I was wearing. He seemed impressed. "Sure," he said, allowing me to snap a few shots with his car. I always carried my Polaroid camera, dreaming of becoming a model. While we finished taking photos, he casually mentioned that he owned the club.

"Have you been to the club before?" he asked.

"No," I replied. "But if you'll allow me, I'd love to hold a fashion show here."

"Come in, let's talk about it," he said, inviting us inside. He gave us a tour and agreed to let us use the club for the show. With his blessing, we organized the event, sold tickets, and put on a fabulous fashion show. LaToya, Sheila, and Cynthia modeled my designs, while I served as the commentator, narrating each garment since I knew them so well.

During this time, my family left Fullerton Street and moved to Manor, near Joy Road. By then, I had been working since I was seven, saving diligently. At nine, I opened my own bank account, with my mom keeping track of deposits. By the time I was 16, I had saved over $1,500. I asked my mom to use my savings to buy me a car, knowing how much I needed one for school. Taking three buses each way was exhausting for a teenage girl.

One day, I came home from school, and Mom said, "Go look in the garage." There it was—a 1965 beige Ford Mustang. My very own car, paid for with my hard-earned money. I was ecstatic! I had already taken driver's ed at Chadsey High School and passed with flying colors. Plus, I had plenty of practice behind the wheel—starting when I was nine, thanks to my dad.

Driving wasn't just a skill; it became a lifeline. Once, when I was 12 or 13, my dad gave my mom a brutal beating, leaving her with two black eyes. The injuries were so severe, we fled the house. I grabbed the car keys from Mom and said, "Get in the car." She climbed into the passenger seat, and I drove us across Detroit to Hubble and Plymouth, where a cousin lived. From there, we went to Henry Ford Hospital. X-rays revealed Mom's cheekbone was fractured, and her swollen eyes were nearly shut. Yet, despite everything, we ended up back with Dad. Mom was the only person I've ever known who truly "turned the other cheek," living her life focused on getting to Heaven.

After getting my car, I ventured out more. One weekend, curiosity led me to 14th Street, where I parked near the 20 Grand Lounge. I was 16, well under the legal age of 21 for drinking or clubbing, but I decided to check it out. At the door, I met a man named CJ and told him I was a seamstress looking for opportunities to showcase my work. I asked if I could hold a fashion show there.

"Hold on," he said, disappearing inside to ask. When he returned, he smiled. "Yes, ma'am. Be here next Friday at 9:00 PM. You'll go on at 10:00."

Thrilled, I called LaToya, Sheila, and Cynthia, who were happy to help. Once again, we poured our energy into creating another show.

After the event, a well-dressed woman approached us, praising our work. She introduced herself as Brenda and was amazed I had made all the garments. Returning to the bar where she'd been sitting, surrounded by men, she invited me over and introduced me to them—most were her uncles. Brenda and I exchanged numbers that night and quickly became close friends.

After moving to Manor Street off Joy Rd I met Yasmin. Yasmin was a couple years older than me, but still a teenager. She lived with her mother and siblings. One day her uncle Justus came to visit his sister, Yasmin's mother. Justus was 24. He was a fine young black man with facial hair. We started dating in 1973. He didn't care about the age difference because I was still only 16. I didn't know what statutory rape was. About six months after meeting Justus, I introduced him to my friend, Brenda. They did not hit it off. Justus gave me an ultimatum to choose either him or Brenda. I chose him and Brenda was so pissed.

My mother's divorce became final in 1973, and we moved again. She got the house back, located on West Grand Ave—the house I was raised in. In the divorce settlement, Dad received the property up North in Woodland Park and the two-family Flat on Vancouver, on Detroit's Westside.

This was a time for change. Justus had other ideas. He wanted to move away from his mother and get an apartment. He asked me to move in with him even though I was still in high school. We sat down and talked about it, and he said, "Take the GED test. If you pass, you can get a job and help with the rent."

I considered this seriously and started classes at a community center located at Dexter and Elmhurst. He scheduled the GED test date, and the class went to the Stevenson building down on Grand River for the test. I was ecstatic when I passed, and the plans with Justus were materializing. He was employed by Ford Motor Co. in Dearborn, and it was a regular routine for me to take him to work and pick him up at 11:00 PM.

I went to Downtown Detroit to look for work and was hired for a job the same day. Shortly after I moved in with Justus, the beatings started. He had an ex-wife and two children. He told me that when he moved out, he gave his Ex-wife the house. Later, he told me that it was his fault because he used to beat her. He said that when he went to Vietnam, he wasn't the same person when he returned. Vietnam took a toll on him, and something would click with him that caused a great rage. He began beating me on a regular basis. The beatings were over little things or even nothing. One time, there wasn't a saltshaker on the table, and another time what to watch on TV was over that night. Justus burned me with a lit cigarette on my thigh. He also put a pot of boiling water with grits and syrup on the stove and threatened to throw it on me. Another time, he held a knife to my throat. He said that he often knew how to beat a woman without leaving marks on her face.

We moved to our second apartment on Davidson Street between Livernois and Petoskey. Justus started selling weed before we left the first apartment. This apartment had a parking lot out back in the alley. He thought this was perfect for business. It was 1974, and it wasn't long before Justus was arrested. He said they told him they had been watching us for a while. He called me at the apartment and told me the police had picked him up that morning. He wanted me to come downtown to 1300 Beaubien Headquarters at the Police Department to bail him out of jail.

I was 17 and still not of legal age. Somehow, I was able to get the money from the bank, and then went downtown to go get him.

To this day, I still don't know how no one recognized that I was just a teenager, a child standing there. When I bailed him out of jail, he told me the lawyer was a Jew with connections to the judge. The lawyer and the judge were communicating and using body language, such as scratching their shoulders or ears. He said he didn't know if they were Mason's or Shriner's, but it was interesting to watch the conversation.

This is a portrait of my father,
Calvin Lilly, Jr.

Deeper into the Streets

A couple of months have gone by. A large yellow envelope came in the mail. It was Justus' mug shots and fingerprints. Justus said they expunged his record. He then started selling weed again and graduated to selling a white powdery substance called Cocaine. At 17, this man was exposing me to weed, and now we are snorting cocaine. If "they" have been watching us for a while, what changed? We can go back to selling weed and go even deeper? Why all of a sudden does Justus want me to engage in unusual sex? Where does all of this come from? I'm still underage, even if Justus is 25. If they have been watching, they have seen me going in and out. Why wasn't he arrested for statutory rape? Why did they let him go when they had him?

I remember many times there were cars of surveillance parked out back with a Caucasian man sitting behind the wheel of the car. He would glance up at me, then quickly look down at a newspaper, then back up at me. There were also two women who would often sit in a car and behave the same, glance downward, and then glance back up at me. I mentioned this to Justus, "Why are there Caucasian people in the parking lot when I go out to my car?" He said, maybe we are being watched. That was saying a mouthful, and he's selling again?

Justus would still beat me up on a regular basis. Often, he would come downtown to my job and beg for forgiveness. I would threaten to leave, and he would shed tears at my workplace, asking me not to leave. I'd go right back to him every time. I was afraid of him, but terrified of leaving him. I was also terrified because I didn't know what my future would be like.

This is a portrait of me and my brother,
Meekie.

Leaving the State

Meekie, my brother, was living in Brooklyn, New York. He calls my mother every week. One day, I happened to be with my mother when he called. He said, "Mom told me about Justus beating you. You should move to New York, get away from that norm, and begin a new life with me." He told me that Justus would not be able to find me because there were so many people there. I was 18 now. I went to work and gave them a two-week notice. I also began writing down the names and addresses of businesses in New York that did business with my employer for job leads. I bought a plane ticket to New York City. I gave my brother the time and date so he could pick me up at the airport.

He said, "My apartment isn't much. I live in a one-room apartment at a Brownstone in Brooklyn. I share the kitchen with an elderly lady, and the bathroom is down the hall. It's a community bathroom. You'll be fine. Just come on. It's in Bedford Stuyvesant."

So, I went to New York City. My brother was there to pick me up at the airport without a car. We took a cab part of the way and got on the subway the rest of the way. My brother put my suitcase in the apartment and then we left again for the subway. No time to rest. Meekie wanted to teach me how to catch the A-train to Manhattan and back. We did two more test runs until I got the hang of it.

Early on a Monday morning, I went to the bathroom down the hall, got dressed and started off for Manhattan to look for a job. One of the names on my list was for a company called

Feature Ring Company. It was half a block from Times Square. I went to the personnel department and told the manager in Human Resources how I got their name and address. I filled out the application and was hired on the spot.

He said, "Can you start tomorrow?"

"Yes sir, I can," I said.

"You'll be working in the wax room with about sixteen other women," he said. "You'll be pulling molds. Wait here, I'll have someone take you up and introduce you."

The supervisor was a tall gentleman named Al. He spoke perfect English. There were sixteen women working in the wax room who did not speak English, and three women spoke broken English.

I would ride that A-Train every morning, M-F, only to catch it daily going back home. There was a meat market at the corner of Herkimer

Street and Nostrum Avenue. I would stop and pick up something to cook for dinner. When it got dark, I would turn off the lights and TV and watch the male prostitutes parade up and down the streets dressed in women's clothing.

One day, I went to the liquor store to buy a lottery ticket. I met a man who worked there. We exchanged phone numbers, only I didn't have my own phone. The only phone in the apartment building was down the hall. The owners of the Brownstone would answer it and relay any messages. The man at the liquor store called me and told me to meet him there. I got dressed and went, because I had no friends. My brother worked in Hoboken, New Jersey. Sometimes, I wouldn't see him for weeks. The man and I talked a long while.

He asked, "Do you go to any Broadway shows?"

"No, I'm new here and don't have any

friends yet," I told him. "Besides, I don't have a proper wardrobe."

"What size do you wear?"

"Size 5 or 7," I said.

A few days later, he called and told me to come to the store. When I met him at the store, he told his boss he'd be right back. He said, "Come with me. I want you to meet my mother." We walked about two blocks over to where he lived at the back of his mother's house. I had a seat on the back porch. He came out of the house with a large black bag full of clothes. The clothes were all on hangers with the price tags still on them. They were all size 5 and some 7's. He told me to try one on and then another. They all fit. Every price tag was over $200. One suit was 100% silk and cost over $400. I looked at him with raised eyebrows. I wanted those clothes so bad. He took me by the hand and sat me next to him. He started kissing me and then said, "You can have them all."

"What am I going to do?" I said to myself.

"Just follow my lead," he told me. One thing led to another, and right there on the back porch, we did the unthinkable. That was the first time I did something like that. I felt dirty, scared, ashamed, and very happy at the same time. Lord, have mercy. It felt good to have quality clothing that cost over $6,000.

This is a portrait of my mother, Evora Lilly.

Crossing the Street in
New York Can Bring Trouble

A couple of weeks went by, and I did not hear from him. The phone rang and Mr. King called out, "Telephone!" It's my friend, Alvin, from the liquor store. He asked if I would come to a club with him for a glass of wine. He told me to dress up in something nice from the clothes he gave me. I got up, made myself sharp, and met Alvin at the liquor store. We walked, and my feet were killing me in the heels that he had bought me. The club was on the same street as the liquor store, four blocks away. The club was rocking with loud music, and people were coming and going. We sat at the bar next to the stage where they had live entertainment. There were two females dressed in leotards from head to toe on the stage, going up and down each other's bodies in a heated, sexual, illustrated motion.

A couple of black men came in, loud and slapping hands and greeting each other with the black man's handshake. My friend introduced me to one of them. His name was Tiger. He and Alvin slapped hands again. Alvin said he was going to the bathroom. "Just sit here and talk to Tiger until I get back." After ten minutes, I started getting worried. I don't know Tiger, and I'm talking with him. Hell, I didn't even know Alvin. The women on stage were interesting to watch, but I'm also getting scared. It had gotten dark.

"Where's Alvin?" I asked Tiger.

"Oh, he's gone," he said.

"What? Gone where?"

"He's gone for the evening."

"Oh My God. I've got to go home. It's dark

out and I don't have a car."

Tiger said, "It's fine. I'll take you home. Where do you live?"

"I don't know you."

"Look at me. I'm a gentleman. Do I look like I would harm you? Look how I'm dressed." He looked sharp and smelled good, too. "Do you think I want to get dirty and mess up my clothes? I don't get physical like that." He assured me I was perfectly safe with him.

"My car is right out front. I'll drop you off and won't even come in," he continued. "But you must give me your phone number and promise to see me again. What other choice did I have? I am in Bedford Stuyvesant at night and only 18 years old. I dropped my head and began praying.

"Come on, are you ready to go?"

"Yes, I'm ready," I hopped off the barstool. He walked me to his car and opened the door for me. He was indeed a gentleman. I gave him the directions to where I lived on Herkimer Street, three blocks up and one block over. He drove me straight to the brownstone, parked out front, and asked, "May I come in?"

"No," I said. "I only have one room." He was nice about it and didn't push the issue.

"Could I call you tomorrow? I'd like to see you again." I said yes.

Tiger waited a couple of days before calling and asking, "Would you like to see the city?"

"Yes, I would." It was daylight when he came to pick me up. We crossed the Brooklyn Bridge and drove to Manhattan. We drove down 42nd Street, Times Square, Madison, 5th Avenue, and much of East Manhattan. We ended up in Harlem, where we stopped and watched people go by.

"Would you like to ride over to my apartment?" he asked me. "I will only be there a few minutes." I was feeling comfortable now, so I said OK. Being young and having left an abusive relationship, this was the first gentleman I had truly met.

We pulled up to a high-rise apartment building located off the Grand Concord. "Please come in. It's dark out and I don't want to leave you in the car by yourself. I assure you, we will only be a few minutes."

"Ok. I'll come in." He insisted I sit in the car until he came around and opened my door. The apartment was a 1-bedroom with a sunken living room. It was the kind of apartment I would love to have. Tiger's cousin lived next door, and his apartment also had a sunken living room. We didn't stay long just as Tiger promised. Coming from an abusive childhood and teenage years, I had never been exposed to much of a stressful street life. Totally green, I had little street sense.

Also, in 1975, when I had first moved to

New York, I had met a man standing in line at LaGuardia Airport who was travelling to Detroit. I was going home to visit my mom. We exchanged phone numbers. He was a singer in a famous singing group from New York. He invited me to the show they were performing in Detroit. He lived on the East Coast of Manhattan. Even though he was a little bit older than I was, we still became friends, although he was more like a mentor. He was genuinely concerned about me.

A Minute of Romance

We were friends for months before I met Tiger. His name was Bubby. I called him and told him I was moving from Brooklyn to the Bronx. I told him I would be staying with a new male friend off the Grand Concord.

"What does he do for a living?" Bubby asked.

"He owns a store in Harlem," I told him, pointing out the store's location and giving him my phone number.

While living with Tiger, I called Brenda's aunt. She was happy to hear from me and said that Brenda lives in Los Angeles now. She gave me Brenda's phone number and we re-united our friendship. Brenda told me about all the celebrities she ran across. It was hard to believe celebrities walk around like common people out there. She invited me to come to LA to live with her. "I have a two-bedroom apartment in the Hills of LA. One bedroom for you, Theresa," she said.

One day, Bubby called me, He said, "Get your ass out of there now."

"Why?" I asked him.

"Don't ask questions. Just do as I say." I guess Bubby had researched the area and found out what products were being sold at Tiger's store.

"Don't worry," I said. "Yesterday, I bought a one-way ticket to LA. I'm moving next week with a friend of mine."

Bubby said, "Get out of there as soon as you can and don't come back."

Tiger took me to the airport on Friday of the following week. I boarded a first-class plane to Los Angeles, California. Brenda was there to pick me up in a brand-new Lincoln. I'm 18 and now living on the West Coast. Brenda pulled up to a high-end apartment in the Hills of California.

It wasn't long before I met an actor named Tony King filming on Sunset Blvd. I also met Cuba Gooding Sr and Flip Wilson. These men have all passed on. Brenda introduced me to her friends, two sisters named Karen and Betrice. Brenda and Karen were best friends. Betrice was a little standoffish. She was very business-minded, whereas the three of us still had a lot of running around in us. One day, Brenda mentioned she wasn't crazy about the friendship that had developed between Karen and me. A fight broke out. Aaron, Brenda's man, was there, and he broke up the fight. But now, I have no place to go. Karen asked Betrice if I could stay with them because Betrice had her own apartment. I was praying because I had no money and didn't know anybody but these two native California sisters. Betrice had a house full. Beatrice's man, Taurus, was there, her sister Karen, and another friend, Kendra. Beatrice said I could stay as long as I paid something on the rent, feed myself, and took care of my own needs.

Well, it wasn't long before I called Tiger in New York and asked him for money to help pay the rent. He sent it for me, and I boarded a plane to go back to New York. I told him I wanted a fur coat like the one I had seen Brenda wearing. I asked him if he would buy me one, and he said yes, he would. He took me down to Delancey Street, where shopping for a fur coat made sense, and he bought me a blue fox fur coat. He had really stepped up to the plate. After receiving the blue fox, I asked him if he would buy one more for Betrice because she had let me stay with her. He bought a silver fox fur coat for her. He also gave me money for my part of the rent.

I went back to LA with gifts and paid my part of the rent. This was only temporary because the rent was not being paid. Betrice hugged me, kissed me, and thanked me. She took the money I gave her to feed her and Taurus. We soon received an eviction notice. We went to stay with other friends of theirs. I made up my mind that I would go back to New York.

After telling Betrice, my friend in New York, kept a briefcase filled with money in his drawer, she wanted to come with me to New York. I asked Tiger if I could bring my girlfriend back with me, and he said yes. Taurus sold the TV and bought Betrice a one-way ticket to NY. Betrice also had help in New York. A friend of hers lived there, and she had other contacts too. She went out one evening with a sharp black man and came back loaded with money. She asked Tiger if she could send for her man and if Tiger would pick him up from the airport and take them to a hotel. He told her yes. Well, I saw my life going nowhere. I asked Tiger if he would send me back to Detroit, and I wouldn't be back. I had to start taking care of myself. That was the last time I saw Tiger

However, my friends from LA became important people in Tiger's life. Two years later, Taurus wrote me a letter from prison and asked if I had talked to Tiger.

"No," I told him.

"We all went to jail," Taurus said. "There were a lot of us. Stay away from him and tell your brother to stay away from him."

I'm Not the Enemy

Also, the government had its hand in it. It was said they locked up everybody, replaced the players, and kept it going. Here it is, decades later, and I find myself plagued by the government nonstop. I discovered they were involved in my life in 1980. We went to war in 1981, and it has been moment to moment ever since. The guy I worked with at Chrysler went to work for the FBI. He said his female cousin also worked for them. He said he was broke, and drove a small black car, but later he came on the scene driving a brand new Lexus. He wanted me to date him exclusively. He said he was tired of being alone and wanted to spend his life with me. But I told him I was complicated and didn't want to date anyone at the time. He pursued me and pursued me. He took me to see the movie "American Gangster." I was shocked, and my jaw dropped when I realized the plot of the movie was like seeing glimpses of my life story flash before my eyes.

As I looked back, I realized there were snippets of the FBI's harassment of my family. At Age seven or eight, coming home from Winterhalter Elementary School, Meekie, my brother, and I walked in numbers with others. Meekie was walking backwards, and he turned quickly and hit his head on the trunk of a very old tree in Russell Woods Park. He had a big knot on his head over his eyebrow, and blood streamed down his face. We rushed home to take care of him. Daddy hadn't made it home from work yet. We heard his car turning at the corner, and we rushed to do our chores. Daddy got out of the car mad as hell, and it showed on his face.

"Why does Meekie have a band-aid on?"

"He was walking backward, turned, and ran into a tree."

Dad was so mad that he beat Meekie. He said he was angry because several Caucasian men at work walked by him and told him, "The dumb son-of-a-bitch walked into a tree." Daddy then said, "They are watching my kids and my entire family."

"They who?" I asked.

Dad never would say. He did tell us he was so pressured at work that he would come home and beat all three of us.

Now, it was coming together. When I was eight or nine, the phone would ring. My father sat next to the phone. It would ring time after time.

"Daddy, aren't you going to answer it?" I asked.

"No and don't nobody else answer it," he said. "Some Caucasian man keeps calling here with the wrong number." Finally, he answered the phone. "Man, you have called here 27 times. Don't no 'Charles' live here. Stop calling my house. Don't call here no more." Dad hung up. Immediately, the phone rang again.

"Don't answer it. It's a Caucasian man playing games on the phone."

It seems this government crap is generational. How far back does it go? Here is what I know . . .

Age 7, my brother runs into a tree

Age 9, the phone rings 27 times—a call looking for "Charlie."

Age 14, a young 16-year-old is found in the rubble

Age 16, birth control pills are too strong for me, resulting in surgery in both breasts

Age 23, my car and apartment were bugged with tracking devices, also with listening and visual devices

Age 24, I met an FBI agent through Yevette

Age 25, I was warned by the FBI on my job at Capper & Capper

Age 26, All-out war between the FBI and me

When I was 25, my friend Yevette invited me over to her house. "Good," I said. "I need to talk to somebody." I drove to her house. "Look at my car. This doesn't look like me. The muffler is just hanging there, and all four hubcaps are gone." I told her. "I want to leave the streets. I'm laid off from Chrysler, but I'm working at a men's clothing store called 'Capper & Capper'. I need help. I'm trying to clean my life up."

"Well, I have friends that are FBI agents," she said. "I could introduce you. They could be the ones to get your life back on track. However, you have got to be sure you are looking for help because once I introduce you to them, there is no going back.

"I want a better life," I told her I've been raped twice in one year and my life has spun out of control. "I need help."

She said OK and made a phone call. Yevette spoke to a man named Charlie Hopkins. "Be right over," he said. It seemed like he was waiting for the phone call. It wasn't long before a man and two women came through the door.

Hi. My name is Charles Hopkins. I'm an FBI agent and Yevette says you want help getting out of the streets."

"Yes."

"What do you do?"

I said, "I sell merchandise illegally."

"What kind of trouble are you having?"

"For instance, look at my car. I'm a neat person and I keep my belongings together. This isn't me." Charles Hopkins asked for my phone number and address.

"We will be in touch with you." He and

one of the ladies with him said. They left.

I went to work the following Monday, downtown at Capper & Capper. Mayor Coleman A. Young came into the store that day through the side entrance. He came over and asked to see some shirts and ties. I assisted him in his shopping spree. He spent $300 and left the store through the front entrance. The back door swung open, and three more people came toward me. It's Mr. Hopkins, another man, and a woman.

"Hello Theresa, remember me? We met over the weekend at Yevette's house." Charles Hopkins said. "Here's my card. This makes it official. Before, you didn't know me from Adam. It says right here 'Federal Bureau of Investigation'. We have been watching you and the building. We noticed Mayor Coleman A. Young has just left out."

"Yes, he did," I said.

"We want you to help us catch him and

another top city official in some wrongdoing."

"No Way!" I said.

"Don't say no. We'll go to lunch or dinner and talk about it."

"Man, I'm not helping you do some shit like that," I said. "You've got the wrong one this time."

"Remember your street hustle," he said. "We'll forgive it, and you will walk free."

"My answer is no."

"Don't rush. Think about it over the week."

"What do I get in return?"

"You will get immunity."

"What is that?"

"You will have to leave the country, change your name, and maybe have plastic surgery." Charles continued. "We'll give you $30,000-$40,000 for a new start in a different country."

"Don't worry about dinner because I won't be going," I said. "My answer is a final no."

"Ok. Just remember the FBI's motto is 'we always get our man'."

I Know

Things Will Get Better

Since that meeting, my life no longer feels like my own. But it doesn't belong to them either—it belongs to the LORD.

I've endured more than I ever thought possible. The FBI's relentless pursuit has left no part of my life untouched. They dig into every account, ruin credit, break you financially, and leave you scrambling just to survive. Their tactics go beyond the obvious. They create distractions, manipulate the IRS, delay mail, and even tamper with medicine—turning a simple prescription into a dangerous gamble.

Poisoned air. Tainted water. Fumes in the car. It's a constant battle.

Mentally, they work to wear you down, pushing you into a state of despair. They're there the moment you apply for housing, ready to block the next step forward. My mother and I have felt their presence even in the smallest of moments—like going to a restaurant, only to walk out sick with ptomaine poisoning.

This is just a fraction of what happens when the FBI takes over your life.

Even ordering medicine is an uphill fight. We always make sure to order Mom's prescriptions early, just to be safe. But the meds never arrive on time. When we call customer service, the response is always vague:

"It should be there tomorrow."

Tomorrow? What about today? What if it doesn't come at all?

"Call your doctor for a 30-day supply. Go to the local drugstore and get it filled."

It's a cycle designed to break us down. We

pay for temporary prescriptions, hoping they aren't tainted. Then the mail-order meds arrive—sometimes good, sometimes not—and suddenly we're sick again. Insurance fights us when hospitalization becomes necessary.

I remember when we ordered an Advair inhaler. Mom took one spray, and within minutes, she couldn't breathe. Poison Control told us not to sleep, to call EMS if it got worse. We ended up in the hospital.

And this started long before now.

When I was sixteen, I was prescribed birth control pills that were far too strong. My cycle stopped entirely for six months. A knot formed under my right breast, deep in my armpit. Alarmed, I showed my mom. She took me to the doctor, hoping for answers. But instead of concern, he prescribed an even stronger dosage—250mg, up from 150mg.

"Did you show them the knot?" Mom

asked when I went to the lobby.

"No, I forgot," I said.

"Go tell the nurse you forgot to show the doctor."

The nurse put me back in the exam room. When the doctor came in I showed him the knot.

"Lay back and stay right there. I'll be back." The doctor returned with two more doctors. They began mashing on both breasts. "The birth control pills are too strong. Take her off them. Talk to her mother. We need to schedule her for surgery." They removed five knots total, so I was told. They removed three knots from my left breast and two from my right. It was torture. I woke up in the recovery room in excruciating pain. My incisions were freshly cut, stitched, and raw. They did not give me anything for pain. I asked for pain medication, and they said I was due to be released soon and couldn't give me pain medication. I know that was a lie. I was given a prescription to get filled on my way home.

Nobody but you, Jesus . . . Nobody but you.

Who were these people that were able to work on my father's nerves to the point that he would come home from work and beat his wife and children? What kind of intelligence would run and say the S.O.B. ran into a tree? Who could set a house on fire with a dead girl of my age inside? Who would break up a family and why? Just how long have "they" been back there? This is a generational curse. They didn't stop at my father. It trickled down through his family. There's evidence of torture to the point of near-death of my mother and brother, all the way down from mattresses full of foreign objects planted inside, to bugging from audio and video devices. The cars were bugged and every house or apartment we ever lived in was bugged. Tracking devices, tainted medicine, fumes through the vents, tainted water... Mom and I would go to sleep, and other things would happen.

"You got the air on?" Mom would wake up and say.

"No, the air is off."

"Well, where is that air coming from?" I'd get up and double-check, and the air would not be on. Poisons were being pumped through the vent. We'd have missing or delayed mail and missing mail-order medicine. "They" are in every aspect of my life.

There is some light at the end of the tunnel. If I can get a good lawyer, I would love to present evidence to the court. I was hospitalized in July 2023 at Stonecrest Behavioral Center. After being released from the hospital, I went to an adult daycare center called "Time Together Adult Day Care Center." At least I was able to find some peace and happiness. Here at Time Together, we do a lot of activities. I was able to get back into my creative side. It's the highlight of my week, and I look forward to coming here. I have made friends here, and the staff makes it very interesting. The owner is a young black lady who ROCKS! Her aunt, who works at the center, is a great help, a great cook, and takes everything as it comes.

Kudos to the entire staff. Everyone pitches in and does their part. Nobody drags their feet. In fact, they all go the extra mile for us.

Now, I am here mainly for mental health and emotional support. Some people are mentally stable, yet some are not. Several group homes come here to the center for mental and emotional help. In fact, there is something here for everyone. We are all here because we all have something not right going on in our lives.

I hope and pray you find this true story interesting. Please stay tuned to my next book, which will have more details. In October 2023, I started talking to two new friends. One lives in NYC, and the other in Los Angeles. They give me educational advice and motivational messages to lift me up. I consider them both to be my mentors.

Until then . . .